EYES HAVE NOT SEEN & EARS]
The First Corinthians 2:
Sherea Rena Gre

G000075486

Copyright 2020: by Sherea Rena Green

Published by Pecan Tree Publishing
Hollywood, FL 33020
www.pecantreebooks.com

Paperback ISBN: 978-1-7372621-0-7
E-book ISBN: 978-1-7372621-1-4
Library of Congress Catalog Number: 2021910053

Cover and Interior Design by: Jenette Antonio Sityar

Pecan Tree Publishing

www.pecantreebooks.com

New Voices | New Styles | New Vision –
Creating a New Legacy of Dynamic
Authors and Titles Hollywood, FL

Contents

Dedication.. vii

Acknowledgements ix

Posthumous Acknowledgements.................................. xi

Introduction xv

Chapter 1: The Family Training Ground 1

Chapter 2: Spiritual and Mental Conditioning............ 11

Chapter 3: Humility...27

Chapter 4: Respect 37

Chapter 5: Giving and Investing of Self..................... 49

Chapter 6: Determination and its Friends..................57

Chapter 7: Mentorship...65

Chapter 8: Can your Birdies Fly? 73

Chapter 9: Succession 79

Chapter 10: Stay Teachable 87

Meet the Author 93

Eyes Have Not Seen & Ears Have Not Heard

The First Corinthians 2:9 Promise

SHEREA GREEN

Dedication

This book is dedicated to my daughter, Tierra Shenate Rossin-Carey.

My life changed 29 years ago when I gave birth to a phenomenal baby girl. Throughout these years, Tierra has inspired and encouraged me. God has given me the opportunity to grow as she has grown. She is an unbelievable DAUGHTER and FRIEND.

I thank God for allowing me to witness my offspring manifest into a fantastic mother, an amazing wife, and a successful pharmacist.

I'm excited about our future. "EYES HAVEN'T SEEN AND EARS HAVEN'T HEARD" Let's SOAR!!!!

Acknowledgements

First, I would like to thank the Almighty for the gift of life and for all the many blessings He has given me. I am nothing without God, and I owe Him my all. For it is in Him and through Him that all things are possible.

Secondly, I would like to thank the most influential women in my life that have helped shape me and guide me along the way. To my beautiful mother, Josephine Morton, what would I do without you holding me down? You've always had my back. Thank you for being my biggest supporter.

My maternal grandmother, Mary Jane Thompson, your prayers still cover me, your teachings and ways continue to guide me. To my paternal grandmother, Henrietta Green-Rozier, thank you for loving me. To my aunt Johnnie Mae Green, you taught me the power of education and the importance of knowing my family roots. You inspired me to reach for more.

I would also like to acknowledge everyone who has been a part of my leadership journey.

I genuinely believe in the power of mentorship, and I know that I would not be the leader that I am without those who have helped me along the way. During my leadership journey, I have been mentored and groomed by some of the best. Thank you for seeing my potential. I was a diamond in the rough, young, shy, and trying to find my way. Thank you for investing in me. Thank you for your wisdom, guidance, and for encouraging me to never settle.

I am truly thankful for the journey. I am most thankful for my legacy of cultivating future leaders. Through my succession planning and mentorship program, I had the opportunity to identify future leaders and create a platform to groom and prepare individuals for the path to leadership within the Broward Sheriff's Office. This in fact, has been one of the most rewarding aspects of my career. To see the fruit of your labor is always a blessing. I have had the opportunity to work with some memorable people. I have learned and grown as a person, as a woman, and a leader. To my subordinates, I know that my no-nonsense reputation preceded me, but you have sharpened me and challenged me. It is because of the lessons I learned while leading you that I am who I am today. It is onward and upward from here. Eyes have not seen, nor have ears heard the things that God has in store.

My mission remains to EDUCATE, ENCOURAGE and EMPOWER as many people as possible with LEADERSHIP, GRIND, VISION and PASSION.

The best is yet to come...

Posthumous Acknowledgements

Elliott Prince, my cousin; you were really my big brother and protector. I miss you dearly and wish you were still here. I know your spirit is still with me. Menesha Prince, my cousin, you were a sister and my best friend. You will never be forgotten.

For lack of guidance a nation falls, but victory is won through many advisers.

—*Proverbs 11:14*

"The purpose of life is not to win. The purpose of life is to grow and to share. When you come to look back on all that you have done in life, you will get more satisfaction from the pleasure you have brought into other people's lives than you will from the times that you out did and defeated them."

—*Harold Kushner*

Introduction

A simple definition of leadership is the art of motivating a group of people to act towards achieving a common goal. A leader is the person in a group that possesses the combination of personality and leadership skills that makes others want to follow their direction.

If you are or desire to be a leader, would you follow you? There are times when I would not have followed me. I was immature, rigid, and I did not listen. I was emotional. I knew nothing about influence. I knew nothing about service, and I most certainly did not know anything about being committed.

Being a great leader, according to a leadership guru I love, John Maxwell, is all about having a genuine willingness and a true commitment to lead others to achieve a common vision and goals, through positive influence. No leader can ever achieve anything great or long-lasting all alone. Teamwork goes hand-in-hand with leadership. Leadership is about people—and for people.

Everyone has talent; however, a good leader possesses the skills to influence others to utilize their talents and be committed to the common goals of the agency or organization. Talent without commitment is just talent.

Maxwell believes, "Leadership is influence, nothing more, nothing less." So, if leadership is influence, you might be asking yourself, "How do I influence others?" Think about someone who positively influenced your life. What behavior or words were so impactful to you that you were influenced to become a better person? What about someone who negatively influenced your life?

What behavior or words did they model and what effect did that have on you?

The point is that influence works positively and negatively. What matters most when it comes to influence is having a positive attitude. Your attitude is contagious, and a positive attitude can shift the entire energy of an organization.

Being a great leader is all about having a genuine willingness and a true commitment to lead others to achieve a common mission, vision, and goals, through positive influence. Just because someone has the title of leader, does not mean they are a leader. The greatest reflection on a leader being a true leader is whether they are influencing anyone. And, of course, the first place you will see that is in the leader's people. An organization is only as great as its people. If the people are not following, the leader is not leading.

So, who am I? Let me introduce Sherea Rena Green. I had the pleasure of serving as, Assistant Director for the Broward Sheriff's Office, Department of Detention, South Operations which includes the Main Jail Bureau, Central Intake Bureau, Court Services, and the Juvenile Assessment Center. I supervised sworn and civilian staff and held a fiscal responsibility to oversee a multi-million-dollar budget.

I am a GRATEFUL, but HUMBLE SERVANT LEADER! In this book, my goal is simple—to share some insight about my philosophies and beliefs on what it takes to be a successful leader. Poured into my thoughts are quotes from speakers, authors, and motivators that I follow faithfully. You will also find biblical teachings woven throughout. I was raised to lean on and respect God and His teaching and they are a cornerstone for who I am—a mother, professional, and leader!!

I ask that God provides each of you with MORE!! More grace, more finance, more mercy, more peace, more joy, more tenacity, more resiliency, more prosperity, more health, more abundance, more favor, and more of God!!

But select capable men from all the people—
men who fear God, trustworthy men who hate
dishonest gain—and appoint them as officials over
thousands, hundreds, fifties, and tens.

—Exodus 18:21

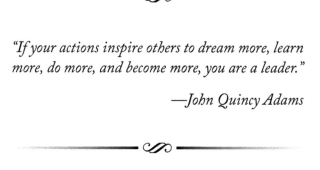

"*If your actions inspire others to dream more, learn more, do more, and become more, you are a leader.*"

—*John Quincy Adams*

CHAPTER 1

The Family Training Ground

I had a wonderful opportunity to begin my journey in law enforcement with the Florida Department of Corrections as a Transfer Clerk. After working in a clerical position, I made the decision to become a certified officer with the State of Florida. This was the beginning of an amazing journey that would take me to places that I never imagined were possible. It was during the formidable years of my career that I began to develop the mindset and fortitude that would lead me all the way to becoming Major Sherea Green.

I was blessed to serve as Captain for the Department of Detention in the Main Jail Bureau in Broward County, Florida. Broward County covers several cities in South Florida and the Main Jail sees a vibrant community of inmates and staff. In December 2019, promotion came, and I took on the position of Assistant Director of South Operations.

Yearning for more, meant it was a necessity to prepare myself with the academic tenacity to meet the requirements for each level of progression I desired. Having a thirst for knowledge and never choosing to settle, I obtained a Master of Science in Criminal Justice in 2006. Thereafter, I acquired several certifications in Leadership Development to remain astute to facilitate my effectiveness and productivity. In the latter part of 2014, I received certification as a Certified Jail Manager and Florida Jail Services Inspector. As an Executive Officer, I was fortunate enough to assist in a one-year preparation for the American Correctional Accreditation (ACA) inspection and Florida Model Jail Standards (FMJS)

It is quite essential to remain vigilant when this degree of responsibilities rest on your shoulders. Having shoulders bold and strong enough to accommodate the weight comes with understanding who you are and what you are called to do. Without doubt, I know that I was called to be a leader. Believe it or not, the training ground began in my family.

As I think back to when I was younger, I remember my mom being a hard worker, employed at Jackson Memorial Hospital in Miami. She worked in histology, assisting in autopsies. Besides working hard, my mom was also thrifty; she did not spend money frivolously.

There were two of us at home with my mom, my brother was seven years older than me. We had a good life, but she was big on saving and establishing credit. Her example of being mindful of your money was one of the earliest pieces of wisdom I gained from her. My mom is also known for her sharp tongue. She is going to tell you how she feels, without hesitation. Yet, she deals with everyone from a big heart. Now my grandmother was sharp on the tongue too, without the profanity my mom could expound on.

One of the core things instilled in me, from both women, was working hard, being ethical in what you do, and again, saving. My family is big on rainy day preparedness. That was a sermon preached often, "Do not spend all your money. Do not spend all your money on unnecessary things. Always think about that rainy day."

We were not that lovey-dovey, overly affectionate family often viewed on 70s and 80s sitcoms. We would come around each other and we would fellowship and have an enjoyable time, but the consistent and genuine expression of love came more through providing the necessary understandings and lessons to live. Becoming a parent illuminated the language of love for me. When I became the mother of a beautiful daughter, I was intentional about not only showing her a lot of love, but it was imperative that love was spoken in words.

It was critical that I assist her in feeling secure about herself and loved by me. Part of my mom's story is that although she had a great and solid foundation, they did not outwardly demonstrate affection. I chose to shift that dynamic. I chose to lead out as a parent differently with my daughter. I witnessed the significant effect that had on my mother. Now she often tells my daughter she loves her. She shows a lot of affection to my daughter even though she is a woman living on her own terms.

Now on my dad's side, it was a bit different. I have four brothers altogether. One brother, my mom's son, and then three brothers who are my father's sons. Unfortunately, two were murdered; and one is in federal prison. He is the brother I was closer to. I knew I did not want the lifestyle I saw through them and around me. Even when I was not sure what road I would travel. One might think that seeing their lives is the reason I chose law enforcement, but it was not. I wanted a more solid foundation for my daughter. I simply always wanted more, even when I did not know what more was.

I know that sounds weird. But many in what could be distressing, or strenuous environments understand that. I knew I did not want to be on the negative list of statistics. I did not necessarily know I wanted to be a leader the way I am now, but I knew I wanted to be something. That is where my mom's and grandmother's work ethics kicked in. I knew I wanted to go to work and make my own money and do the right thing.

I think my brothers' struggles and interactions with the communities around us sparked an interest in law enforcement and I allowed that interest to steer me in that direction. My youngest brother was murdered at age 19. Because we did not live in the same household, we were not that close. My other brother was in the streets a lot. So, we would see each other here and there, but we really were not that close. He was about 40 when he died. I would try to talk to him about his lifestyle. Unfortunately, the streets won the battle.

Their lifestyles, what I saw in school and the areas around me, and the struggles I witnessed impressed upon me to think critically about how I wanted my life to be.

I became a mom at the age of 21. I knew that I wanted a better life for us and did not want to be in a financial position that I would continue to need welfare. Until one day, when my daughter was about a year old and I was in a store getting ready to pay for groceries and I saw this guy standing in line. He looked like he had money. He was dressed in a uniform. I watched him as he walked out to his car. He got into a nice car and I said, "Hmm, I should look into what he does as a career."

I did some research and I found that he was a corrections officer. I wanted to be able to have the wonderful things I saw in his possession that day and from what I could determine, being a corrections officer could allow me to afford those things. The challenge was—I was scared to become an officer because I was terribly shy. But you never allow an obstacle to stop you. You find a way to tell it to move. So, I applied and began my career in 1993 as a clerk typist. In 1995, about three years after my daughter was born, I gained enough confidence to become a corrections officer.

That lack of confidence began at an early age. I remember growing up feeling like I did not belong in a status quo situation, and I also remember playing with my grandmother's China when everybody else was outside. My uncle would often tease me about how much time I spent with those fragile dishes. He and the rest of the family knew I was different, but you know what they could say. Transparently, my mother's family (who I grew up with) were facing several generational and societal struggles. I found my space away from that while still being a part of it.

I inherited more of the characteristics of my father's family. They are all educators; thus, they were big on education. They were big on family as well. Although, I did not have a close relationship with my father, I knew who he was, and he knew me. One of the keen things I gleaned from my paternal side is accountability in the way business was conducted, as well as organization. Regardless of your family dynamics, there is something to be learned and applied productively. From my mom's side of the family, I gained street knowledge. That knowledge benefitted me, especially in the line of work that I am in. I know certain things and that sharpens my discernment. Being around my father's siblings, I know that I can have that seat at the table and negotiate the seat I have.

So many times, members of my family automatically expect me to be in a leadership role. It can be anything, from family reunions to trips. This is seen in both families. The dynamics maternally shifted when my grandmother passed in 2014. While I have tried, to some degree, to fill her leadership role in family bonds remained strong, that has been difficult. Having her grand sense of love for a family with a positive outlook, I make sure my daughter sees and understands my leadership role as her mom and available, wise counsel.

I was strict with my daughter. I held her accountable. I was very transparent with her. She knew my expectations. She knew that failure was not an option and that she had to try extra hard. When my daughter was younger, she had bad ear infections that affected her speech. Doctors said she probably would never speak clearly. I could not accept that. So, I spent a little money and bought the Hooked-on Phonics program that was once popular and widely televised. I purchased every series they had. Day after day I would sit at the table and I would work with her. We worked together until I taught my baby to read. I was determined not to leave her under a grim prognosis. When we were not working on her speaking and reading, she was dancing, so, I enrolled her at the famed Edwin Holland School of Dance in Miami. I knew that dance would help her develop her concentration skills and discipline. These were two components she would lean on as a student in the nationally recognized school of pharmacy at Florida Agricultural and Mechanical University (FAMU). She is now a pharmacist. We frequently talk about expectations and her vision.

The leadership gene that shows up in young people may not almost look like leadership. It may look like bossiness, extreme curiosity, or being in the way. Before you allow the stigmas to dictate how they are directed, try something different. Activities that sharpen discipline, concentration, logic, problem-solving and those things that seem contrary to their behaviors. Family is the first training ground for the leaders that will hold key positions in our lifetime. Family was the initial place where I learned a mantra I continue to live by: It is better to give than to receive; giving begins the receiving process.

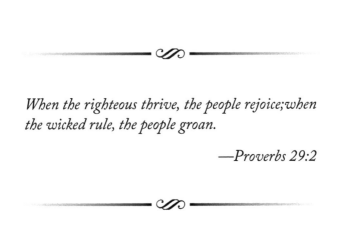

When the righteous thrive, the people rejoice; when the wicked rule, the people groan.

—Proverbs 29:2

Everybody can be great...because anybody can serve. You do not have to have a college degree to serve. You do not have to make your subject and verb agree to serve. You only need a heart full of grace. A soul generated by love."

—*Martin Luther King, Jr.*

CHAPTER 2

Spiritual and Mental Conditioning

Deepak Chopra, author, advocate, and motivational speaker wrote, "Enlightened leadership is spiritual if we understand spirituality not as some kind of religious dogma or ideology but as the domain of awareness where we experience values like truth, goodness, beauty, love and compassion, and also intuition, creativity, insight and focused attention."

Everything in one's life must be built or established on a firm, steady and certain foundation. Some may believe that philosophy only applies to major decisions or milestones. That is not the case. Every step, decision, movement, and thought that comes through you and must be made by you must come from a steady and assured place. Without a doubt that steadiness comes from your spiritual and mental capacity. If the two are in disarray or are absent critical thinking and proficient decision making will suffer.

In her study for BIOMEDICAL REPORTS, a Spandidos Publications study, "Spiritual leadership at the workplace: Perspectives and Theories", author Yishuang Meng wrote: "Two essential elements of spirituality include: i) Transcendence of self which usually manifests in a sense of calling or destiny, and ii) belief that one's activities have meaning and value beyond economic benefits or self-gratification. Development of certain values, including vision (for example, developing a definition of destination, reflection of high ideals, and encouraging the hope/ faith emotions), altruistic love (e.g., forgiveness, kindness, integrity, empathy, honesty, patience, trust and humility), and hope/faith promotes a sense of calling and higher meaning."

Ming also notes that a successful model of spirituality in leadership and in workplace leadership comes through a spiritual and principle-based model by Stephen Covey, "Principle-centered leaders willingly serve (calling) others while keeping the harmony with natural laws and principles. These leaders are guided by the seven habits that enable them to renew harmony and maintain balance in the background of constant changes and external pressures. These habits drive them to keep learning, value first, believe in others, radiate positive energy, face life as an adventure, be synergistic, lead balanced lives, and renew through exercise."

Covey models what many in religious circles call servant leadership.

WHAT IS A SERVANT LEADER?

A servant leader's focus is on serving others rather than serving themselves or being served by others. A servant leader meets people where they are at so they can climb to the top alongside them rather than charging ahead. Maxwell wrote that his shift into a servant-leadership role happened when "[he] started to change his leadership focus to empowering others to do what [he] was doing." Servant leaders do not want to be successful all on their own. Servant leaders are looking to build a team not an empire, because they know once they build the team, success follows.

"When you decide to serve others as a leader, the team's success becomes your success."

—John C. Maxwell

There are some key habits that will help you become a servant leader. Leadership Expert John Maxwell says those habits include:

➢ Accountability
➢ Open and honest communication
➢ Transparency (No secrets)
➢ Honesty and Integrity
➢ Consistency
➢ Inspire Others
➢ Commitment and Passion

➢ Be thankful for the small things
➢ Be a better Servant

Characteristics of Being a Godly Leader, connected to solid spiritual and mental foundations include:

• Recognizing the value in other people and continually invests in others
• Good character
• Not self-promoting
• Uses their influence for the good of others
• Has laser focus on the vision
• Serves others expecting nothing in return
• Is accountable towards others; I always tell my team that I will hold them accountable and I expect them to hold me accountable

There is an alignment of the principles that Meng and Covey indicate are key in the spiritual and mental conditioning of an excellent leader. A biblical verse that I reflect on often to remind of the importance of selflessness and valuing others above myself, so that I am better positioned to make a real impact is Philippians 2:3. The New International Version (or translation) of that scripture reads,

*"Do nothing out of selfish ambition or vain conceit.
Rather, in humility value others above yourselves."*

The mental conditioning allows me, as a leader, to think and guide from another perspective. I think that's also part of a leader's duty, helping their team become mentally conditioned to not only do a better job but to look at their professional development. Part of being a leader is understanding not only your own thought process but the mental conditioning of those you are leading. It is impossible to do that without some practices and rituals in place to conditioning the person within, so that the person who shows up externally does so holistically well and powerful.

I make sure I exercise vigorously and consistently, so that physically I am prepared to face challenges, directives and schedules that can easily create physical exhaustion. If I am not in good health and I am not feeling well, how do I lead? So, I must exercise, I juice, I eat right, I protect my thoughts.

Here is what my mental conditioning routine looks like; and it is purposely structured so that I can gain the ultimate results. I awake at 4:30 in the morning to go to the gym and I work out for about an hour. From the time I open my eyes, as I am driving to the gym, as I am working out, I am listening to something to motivate me. I listen to my mentors, Zig Ziglar, Les Brown, TD Jakes, Joel Osteen, Grant Cardone, and John Maxwell. My motivation playlist changes from time to time so that I have varied styles and perspectives to pull from. Most of those I listen to are centered on the themes of spirituality/God, leadership, and mental/emotional stability.

I listen to motivation and powerful thoughts until the time I begin my workday. That is about three hours EVERY weekday morning, and sometimes on the weekends.

When I am not listening in my car, I am praying. I am having my casual conversation with God. My conversation is simple, and an example is, "Lord, thank you for this day. Thank you for great decision-making skills Lord, thank you for covering my people Lord God, thank you for always giving me an opportunity to lead. Thank you for giving me the opportunity to represent You; and Lord, what do You want from me today? Who do You want me to touch today? Drop it in my spirit. Keep my eyes on You, Father. Keep me humble. Let everyone that interacts with me see You though me."

I journal first thing every morning. Part of my journaling process is writing the things I am thankful for and the latter part of my journaling is planning my day/week/month/year/decade. I am writing how my day will be. I may jot down today; I am going to create a great global vision plan. Today, I am going to reach out to a resource and learn something that is going to impact the world, when I intentionally do this, I am setting my tone. I am setting my mindset. I am conditioning my mind. I am practicing mental preparation. Most importantly, I plan my day at the beginning of my day, and as I do I prepare for my future. As Bishop T.D. Jakes, Founding Pastor of The Potter's House teaches I am planning my decade and speaking what it will hold for me.

What started all of this for me? I knew I wanted better and more. I did not know how to get it or if I was strong enough to handle it. There was a time I did not do anything. I did not go to the gym; I would pray here and there. I would go to church here and there, but I was not consistent. Let me note here, that while I am speaking from a Christianity perspective, whatever your spiritual/religious belief – if it is good, positive, life giving and affirming, teaches giving a portion of what you have to a place of worship or charity (tithing), you should be consistent in practicing it. Not only for your benefit but for the benefit of others.

One day I was listening to one of Bishop Jakes' sermons discussing commitment. His focus was on being genuinely and completely committed; not just saying what you are going to do but really doing it and being consistent in those things you give your word to. I knew that if I wanted things to change; (and God had already started showing me what He could do for me) I had to be mentally ready to not only receive it but to obtain it, and to continue to move on. I may have wanted to be a Major, (I was a Captain at the time), but was I ready to be a Major?

Was I mentally ready to take on the task? The fall of 2019 the world became inundated with the awakening of COVID-19.

By 2020, it had fully invaded America and several other countries. God knew something about me during that season of desiring to be a Major. There was still some personal and leadership preparation I needed to undergo. I needed to be fully committed to what I was asking for. We did not know the Coronavirus was coming. What I do know now, is there is no way I could have handled the pandemic in my position as an Assistant Director. There is no way that I could have overseen the division had this happened a year earlier. I was able to manage it so much better because I was more mentally and spiritually prepared and grounded. I grew mentally exhausted, but I was able to handle it better and I learned resiliency.

God helped me to get here with mental and physical conditioning. Because just like my mental preparedness, my body did better condition to the stressors that come with global, sudden, or other dramatic and traumatic shifts.

One of the wonderful things about my perspective and ways that I create and operate through my mental and physical conditioning; is sharing it with my team. Every Monday, I met with my key people, the people that report directly to me, and I explain to them that the meeting is twofold. Seventy percent of the meeting is to make sure that they are good, because we get so busy in the hustle-and-bustle of life and the hustle and bustle of trying to get the job done, that we do not really take time to make sure we are good. So, it was important that I look at them (prior to COVID). I wanted to make sure their physical being was good and make sure they were okay.

Part of my responsibility as a leader is not only to speak up if I see that one of my team members is having challenges, but to help. There are so many different components to leadership and knowing that your team is feeling a level of confidence so they can produce, is paramount to crossing the finish line. My team's area of service was crazy busy, and they got the job done proficiently; but that does not always mean that they were doing well in their own space inside of the job or outside. Some days I would suggest, "Restructure your schedule today." Or I would encourage, "Delegate tasks that are taxing for you to get to and we will disseminate the work to other stakeholders." Or, maybe I would take on the task, and most of the time they would say they have it. I think they knew that their well-being was important to me. It provides better work product. I intentionally focus on keeping my mental conditioning strong and encouraged them to do the same.

One of my favorite authors and speakers to engage is John Maxwell. His leadership style is one that I want to emulate. He brings a spiritual aspect into leadership. He has time for compassion. He is a servant leader and that is important to me. He opened my perspective on leading and serving through his understanding of living your purpose by reaching for something bigger than yourself. It is about who you are called to be in place for!

One of the most important parts of leading a team and knowing each team's strengths and weaknesses, what it takes to maintain stability and what is necessary to change if that stability begins to disconnect. It is vital that each team member, each person working in ministry or an organization, and each family member knows this about each other. Let me explain. Understanding that the team members need leadership from each other, being able to guide others and remain focused. Iron sharpens iron. For this reason, part of my leadership spiritual and mental condition is regular self-checks. That self check includes how what is going on with me is affecting my team. If each of us does that, then we can better understand each other to create smooth workdays and transitions.

I knew the strengths and weaknesses of each person that reported directly to me. Even if the people that report directly to you are your children you still must lead them individually as well as collectively. If someone in my family called me today and said I need assistance; I know which family member can lead out in helping. If someone called me right now and said, "I need this done on a project" I know who to call and get it done, and why they are going to be effective at it. Think about those on your team. You may have a young man who is a get-it-done type of guy. He is what you would call a foot soldier. If you tell him to walk to the grocery store in three steps, come back in four steps, go around the corner twice, he is going to do that with precision; when you or someone on the team needs a job done that requires someone who can follow detailed directions towards completion, he is your go-to person. He is not going to ask, "Who? What?" He is going to get the job done. It is imperative that you know your team and their talents. So much time could be saved knowing your team's abilities; because when things are on the fire you don't have the time to go through the files and figure out who can, who cannot, who might, who will not.

People also have individual ways of responding to a leader's requests or expectations. And so, when you address someone about their emotional and mental responses as a leader, this can be a challenge; that is why you must know your team's story – their capacity. I keep going back to this because the way that a message is conveyed to and from and received to Person A may hit diametrically opposite to Person B.

I had to work on this because I am a direct person because that is how I prefer to receive communication – directly. Do not take me around the corner and across the street, do not sugar coat it or dress it up. If I messed up, just say "Sherea you messed that up. You did not handle that properly." Then I am ready to apologize if necessary, correct if needed, and move onto the next thing. But I understand everybody is not like me. Understanding to some degree the spiritual and mental strength of those you lead and serve with help you refine those things that you expect of yourself that you project on others.

I have team members professionally and personally, who can receive information the way I can. I can be very direct, "Hey, I need you to do this and then get back with me." But there are some people that cannot handle that. Some people need to understand the why and what so that they can process it. Then I must recount some things because if I do not, they do not receive it well; they do not do the follow up well and they take it personally. Situations such as these require a certain thought process for the leader. This is the perfect example where leaders, would be responsible for not only thinking through their response but how it should be delivered. I pride myself on being a transparent leader. There is no communication too big to share with the team. When I communicate, I encourage two-way, open, and honest feedback. That – is how we all grow.

I think as people, we do not realize how profound our thoughts are. Think about it. A microwave oven or a car started as a thought. Our phones and wireless technology commenced with thoughts. So, one of the things that I pray for every day is, "God, bring me positive, creative, courageous global thoughts. Bring me out of the box thoughts and thinking." I do not want to be just average. I do not want to just get up and just go to sleep at night. Throughout my days, because we do not know how many days we have here, I want every day to be an asset for me and for those I encounter. So, I always bring what I hope are engaging and insightful thoughts to the table. And most of the time I will suggest something. It is important that you voice your thoughts and ideas. Your voice has value. There have been times lead staff has been on conference calls, I will say something that I really did not think was big. I just throw it out there. Someone will respond, "Oh my God, that was such a great thought!" All the while I am thinking, "Okay;" but you know I prayed for that, right?" God bring me good thoughts.

We must focus on our thoughts and not take thoughts for granted; because THAT thought you push down or do not express could be designed to take you to the next level or to place you only see in your private space. If you are a negative person and your thoughts are always negative, that is what you create in your life. Your glass will remain half empty, until you start having full glass thoughts. And start speaking or writing full glass in a custom-designed kitchen. So, pray for full thoughts. I want to always take it to a different level. I want to always have positive thoughts. I am trying to shift from negative thoughts all together even though we have them at times, I am trying to work on not having them overtake my time or any situation. So, I am always declaring, "God, bring me good thoughts. Create a positive powerful mindset for me."

Oh, but God is humorous. He helps me create a positive mindset to prepare me to assist and lead others who may not be as positive, even on my team, in the various community organizations in which I serve, and in my family. Fortunately, my teams – across the board - understand my expectations. And if anybody comes to the table with negativity, I will ask them, "Why do you feel like that?" If somebody says, "Well let's try this" and the team responds negatively, I must shift perspectives. I would prefer, "Well, how do we know if we never tried it?" We will try everything. They call me the "Pilot Queen" because I facilitate a lot of pilot initiatives. My team will try everything if it leads us on a good path. If it does not work - it was a pilot - at least we tried it. At least we put our heads together, because we must put our heads together, to help an idea manifest. If we shoot down somebody's thoughts or their ideas of something that they bring to the table because we do not think it is right, that is unfair. And how do we ever progress? How do we ever become change agents if we never try anything?

I strongly encourage my team to be change agents. They cannot just throw out an idea, they must conduct processing; how is it going to work, the weaknesses, the strengths, the cons/pros, and expenses. You must lead this type of idea processing and development from a place of calm and certainty though; otherwise, things can run amok. To help this processing operate as smoothly as possible, I have also incorporated meditation into my personal and work life.

If I know I have a meeting with my team at one o'clock, no later than about 12:45 I am trying to shut everything down. I am not looking at emails. I already have my notes out and I am mentally preparing. My conversations, my dialogue with God come into play again. We have conversations all throughout the day. This time that conversation sounds like, "You know Lord, this will be a good meeting. Thank you for the great ideas that are manifesting. We are going to walk away with three things that we are going to try. Lord, control my emotions, my facial expressions. Please let me be patient with those that say things that I do not necessarily agree with. Let the team know that I am here, that they can trust me." I mentally shift and prepare for my meeting.

Even with all your plans as a leader with a team, encouraging the strengthening of one's mind and spirit works for some, but does not work for others. Everybody is not going to like your leadership style, but if it is a style that is meant to challenge, empower, and invigorate those you lead in any capacity – hold true to it. There are some people who do not like my leadership style and that is okay if I know I am doing the right thing, then I am good. My goal is to get everybody on board based on the vision and mission ahead and their capacity.

As a leader, I must be able to be honest with team members when it comes to their performance and learning how to complete new tasks or duties. Differences makes us unique, however, those same differences can make strife if not approached appropriately. Respect is key. We do not all think alike, and we have different type of mindset, because I do not want everybody to think like me. We are not going to really progress if we think in that way. So, I think everybody must have different mindsets as well when you are at the table.

You need cultural and ethnic diversity, and you need men and women. The perspectives help us to enlarge and expand our thinking and understanding of those sharing the world with us. That makes us unique. If you can create a dynamic of equality and equity within your team then you can organically begin to create that in every circle connected to you because you see it in action and you know that it makes a powerful impact. Will challenges arise? Certainly, but as Bishop Jakes teaches, "Problems are gymnasiums for our faith to work out in. You will never build up strength without resistance."

All this still has a connection to the mental. It is so important for leaders to focus on their mental conditioning, and here more reasons to support this belief. An emotional leader is a poor leader. The temperature of your team is built on the leader. During the pandemic, I challenged my sergeants to remain steady and calm; I did so using a flight analogy. When you are on a plane and you go through turbulence, if the pilot is calm, you are calm. In fact, you have a seat and put on your seatbelt. But if you have a pilot who is panicking, every passenger on that flight will be in an uproar. That is also what happens with an emotional, unbalanced, unconditioned (spiritually and mentally) leader – the passengers are tossed to and from based on the environment that comes from their emotions. I must work on myself because I get hit with a ton of things simultaneously. When I walked in that building to lead my team, I had to be right. So, if I do not meditate, if I don't journal, if I don't pray, if I don't listen to my spiritual music, there is no way I can deal with those problems and not be emotional. Now, I am not saying I do not have my moments here and there because I do. When I do however, I go right back to the things that keep me inspired and grounded.

I believe that there is a place where spiritual and mental training and leading from that place that has been lost in more contemporary times. We must relearn how to be home with and sit around as a family and go back to the basics of praying, praying as a family. We must practice caring and compassion as God does with those we serve with and lead. Some of the things I do to practice team care is send personal birthday messages, pick up the phone, call, listen, and console if a staff member is facing bereavement, check on them directly if they have been injured or are out sick. And it is not about "when will you be back at work;" it is about I know right now you need me to care. I want you to know that I do.

God will never leave me or forsake me; and I believe that. Reflecting Him in my actions is a part of my lifestyle. I believe He is never going to put more on me than I can bear even if I feel like I can't, I know He is going to give me that extra burst of energy and strength to take me through. I believe that. Every leader needs to have something or someone bigger and mightier than them to believe in and cling to.

"Do nothing from selfish ambition or conceit, but in humility count others more significant than yourselves."

—*Philippians 2:3-4*

"*Doing nothing for others is the undoing of oneself. We must be purposely kind and generous, or we miss the best part of existence. The heart that goes out of itself gets large and full of joy. This is the great secret of the inner life. We do ourselves the most good doing something for others.*"

—*Horace Mann*

CHAPTER 3

Humility

"When choosing a leader, we always kept in mind that humility provides clarity where arrogance makes a cloud. The last thing we wanted was to be led by someone whose judgment and actions were clouded by arrogance." The Lakota Indian Way.

"Being humble means recognizing that we are not on earth to see how important we can become, but to see how much difference we can make in the lives of others." Gordon B. Hinckley, author, and American religious leader.

The academic definition of humility from the Cambridge Academic Content Dictionary is: "the feeling or attitude that you have no special importance that makes you better than others; lack of pride." As I embrace humility and strive to walk in it, I lean to a more spiritual description. The Bible describes humility as meekness, lowliness, and absence of self. The word humility in the biblical text of Colossians 3:12 is translated from a Greek word which means "lowliness of mind." That text (don't worry this will not be a sermon, but it helps me paint a vivid understanding) reads, "Therefore, as God's chosen people, holy and dearly loved, clothe yourselves with compassion, kindness, humility, gentleness and patience.

We see that humility is a heart attitude, not merely an outward demeanor. One may put on an outward show of humility but still have a heart full of pride and arrogance. Jesus said that those who are "poor in spirit" would have the kingdom of heaven (Matthew 5:3) Being poor in spirit means that only those who admit to an absolute bankruptcy of spiritual worth will inherit eternal life. Therefore, humility is a prerequisite for the Christian. Humility is also a prerequisite for the leader. Look at what a humble leader already possesses: compassion, gentleness, patience, meekness, absence of self (non-arrogant), not prideful.

There is no greater example of humility in the entire Bible or any leadership model (in my humble opinion) than you find in Jesus Christ. Whether you believe to be The Christ like I do, or one of the prophets this is true. The Apostle Paul writes of Christ's ability to lead with humility as a mandate for those seeking life wisdom, "Do nothing from selfish ambition or conceit, but in humility count others more significant than yourselves. Let each of you look not only to his own interests, but also to the interests of others" (Philippians 2:3-4). I am glad Jesus didn't look to His own interests because He prayed three times in The Garden to have the cup removed from Him, so Paul admonishes us to "Have this mind among yourselves, which is yours in Christ Jesus, who, though he was in the form of God, did not count equality with God a thing to be grasped, but emptied himself, by taking the form of a servant, being born in the likeness of men" (Philippians 2:5-7). What if Christ said, "No one else is being crucified who is innocent? Why do I have to die, I didn't do anything," instead, "being found in human form, he humbled himself by becoming obedient to the point of death, even death on a cross" (Philippians 2:8). Jesus gave up the glory He had in heaven. He gave up His place on the throne where God rules the universe. He gave up His power to defend Himself but willingly gave His life as a ransom for many (Mark 10:45). He loved us so much that He died for us. He endured such shame, ridicule, scorn, torture, humility, and an agonizing death on a cross.

I must take it back to Him and I go for that level of humility. Sir Isaac Newton once noted, "If I been able to see further than others, it is because I have stood on the shoulders of giants." That is why I look to such a powerful leadership example as Jesus. If I am standing on His humble shoulders, not only do I see through a giant's vision, but I see it for more than me. Then I understand that my shoulders should be braced and prepared for standing on.

There are things that weaken the platform of humble shoulders – ego, arrogance, indifference, unconcern, and vanity. You cannot allow your arrogance and ego to dictate how you stand before others and lead them. Because certainly you do not lead them, you harangue them into action by dangling carrots dipped in diamond and platinum as proof of your accolades. You must stay away from the ego. I am thankful that I was able to obtain the rank of Major. I am thankful because no one could have ever told me that I would obtain this level of success in my life. I, and my achievements are such much deeper than a car, or the big house. This is God reminding me, "I am just letting you know you could be a Major, but I got something bigger for you. What impact are you going to have on the team to show them that?" My goal is that when other's see me, that they do not look at me but see God through me. I want them to seek a closer relationship with God. So, if I just get it right with God, then He can do this for you too." We do not have to compete, manipulate, scandalize, or throw dirt on one another. Believe it or not there is good success and multiple accolades for each of us, without us grabbing one and then lording it over others.

Take away the material stuff and the lofty titles and what are you left with. What about great relationships? What about amazing friends on your journey? What about peace of mind? What about good health? You can have a whole lot and be sick physically, emotionally, relationally, and psychologically. For me it means more to have the intrinsic, emotional, and spiritual success. It meant something to put on my uniform and walk in the jail and echo, "Good morning everybody, how are you doing?" My hair is done, the makeup is on, and I am holding it together with all the stresses and all the chaos of the position. God wants us to focus on Him and how He is. There is too much of self-going on and we must get out of ourselves to take on the essence, personality, and characteristics of Him. That is when we can be fully humble, fully powerful, and fully great leaders.

In an October 2018 article on Forbes.com, Author and Leadership Strategist Jeff Hyman wrote, "I suspect that humility gets a bad rap because it is sometimes linked with subservience or weakness or introversion. Psychological research indicates the opposite. Humility is most strongly associated with a cluster of highly positive qualities including sincerity, modesty, fairness, truthfulness, unpretentiousness, and authenticity. And there's nothing about humility that makes it incompatible with strength and courage."

In the article, Hyman lists several questions that one should consider in assessing a candidate's sincere humility. I would argue that the questions are key for determining the level of humility a leader possesses as well. Those questions are: "Do they credit others? (or choose not to acknowledge the contribution of others); Do they admit to mistakes? (and seek to understand and correct what was done/said wrong); Do they accept constructive feedback? (or blame and pass the fault); Do they strive to overcome their weaknesses? Do they help others?

I would add some questions to the list: Do you have to always be in charge? Can you allow someone else to lead and you serve? Can you applaud someone for achieving a goal you had in mind? Do you affirm those around you? Do you encourage and applaud those around you? Can you be a part of a conversation and not turn the conversation to you or a personal experience?

Bold Business, in a September 2018 online article pondered, "Why is humility so important when it comes to effective leadership? For one thing, humble leaders decrease power distances between themselves and others. For another, despite being in leadership positions, humble leaders acknowledge their mistakes and weaknesses. As a result, they appear "more human"— consequently, others easily relate to them more. Also, humble leaders ask others for advice and feedback, and they practice transparency when they share information. As a result, humility and leadership together foster trust and respect while empowering people to be their best. All these things enhance team creativity and organizational performance."

Many leadership strategists and gurus often speak of Chik-Fil-A founder Truett Cathy when it comes to proof that humility and business and financial success go hand-in-hand. Truett often talks about and exemplifies that effective leaders can place the needs of others before theirs (and potentially the organization), and he's built encouraging the growth and improvement of staff on every tier into the company model, plus we all know their service to customers is paramount. Rarely does he talk about the company's success without the stories of those who have succeeded as team players, managers, and corporate leaders at the forefront. That is how humility leads.

The Bold Business article also pointed to another exemplary humility model. "Cheryl Bachelder is another great example of a modern leader who believes in humility. Bachelder took over as CEO of Popeyes in 2007 after the company had declined significantly. Immediately, she became what she called a 'servant leader' and shifted the company's attention to looking at the needs of others. This decision not only pertained to customers but to employees and franchisers as well. By being humble, reaching out to others for feedback and being open to change, Bachelder demonstrated evident humility and leadership.

Truly, humility is an important way to show others that we value them and honor their presence. As I was dreaming one night, I was overwhelmed by a spirit of gratefulness and humility. I was praising God for all the amazing things He has done in my life. In this dream, I was running and jumping, and sending praises up to my Father for His FAVOR!

Out of nowhere God appeared and hugged me so tight and whispered in my ear, "My daughter, thank you for your faithfulness; if you think you are grateful now, just wait because EYES HAVE NOT SEEN AND EARS HAVE NOT HEARD WHAT I HAVE IN STORE FOR YOU; just remain faithful and humble."

I awoke in tears because the dream appeared to be so real. Every day for the next seven days, I was blessed tremendously. I was showered with an abundance of treasures with my health, finances, real estate, and a promotion. God picked me, out of everyone, HE PICKED ME! What I learned from that dream and other experiences is that there is nothing too big for God. He just wants us to trust Him in all things and not lean on our own understanding. Now, the road has not always been a bed of roses; however, I always shift towards positive results and this is because of God's FAVOR! "In humility value others above yourselves, not looking to your own interests but each of you to the interests of the others." – Philippians 2:4.

And David shepherded them with integrity of heart; with skillful hands he led them.

—Psalm 78:72

"The greatest day in your life and mine is when we take total responsibility for our attitudes. That's the day we truly grow up."

—*John Maxwell*

CHAPTER 4

Respect

"When we treat people merely as they are, they will remain as they are. When we treat them as if they were what they should be, they will become what they should be." Thomas S. Monson. Embracing the content of this quote, has enabled me to pave a phenomenal path for my family and most important a phenomenal path for me. I learned this valuable lesson when Tierra (my daughter) graduated from high school and was preparing to attend Florida Agricultural Mechanical University.

My family planned a birthday/trunk party and during the May 2010 extravaganza, I told a story that began with my pregnancy and shifted to a journey that I imagined she would take after the party and she was on the road. I shared how Tierra's college years would shift into her adult years. I was so specific with my story. I detailed how she would be stressed out and would call me to talk her off the bridge several times (not literally, but hopefully you understand the messaging). I shared how she would call me to pray for her and no matter what I was engaged in, I would immediately stop and pray.

The exact sentiments shared that day unfolded. Words are so powerful, she would, in fact, always call at interesting times. I remember driving to work, late for a meeting and guess what? The phone rings and it is Tierra, sharing that the curriculum was way too much, and she could not do it anymore. "Mom I just can't!" As promised, I pulled my car to the side of the busy highway and prayed for God to comfort her and strengthen her mindset. I asked that He walk alongside her during times of distress. Well, you know how that conversation ended. "Mom I appreciate and love you," and our day continued. I must share that we had many conversations like that. I did not realize that her situation was preparing me for my situation. Faith is taking the first step even when you do not see the whole staircase...I am excited to witness the end of her story.

You are wonderfully made with no real guidance or mentorship; however, you hold talent that will leave a unique legacy. Your shyness will transform into you being one of the greatest speakers that has graced this universe. Your arduous work will transform into you being a change agent. Your respect comes from your compassion and understanding the importance of understanding a person's story. A person's story tells the world who we are; why we eat the way we do, talk the way we do, respond the way we do, RESPECT is EVERYTHING and EVERYTHING is RESPECT!!

I believe my daughter's respect for me manifests from her knowledge of my connection with the Holy Spirit. Colossians 3:15, "Let the peace of Christ rule in your hearts, since as members of one body you were called to peace. And be thankful," shows us that peace acts as an umpire for our decision making. Peace or lack thereof about something is a way the Holy Spirit helps to guide our next step. The Holy Spirit can help us build mutual respect when we trust Him to help us focus on one another's strengths rather than weaknesses.

God has given each person special strengths, abilities, and gifts which are unique to that individual. Rather than focusing your attention on what someone else lacks, trust the Lord to help you highlight their God given positive qualities. Paul wrote, "Think about things that are pure and lovely, dwell on the fine and good things in others, think about all the things you have to praise God for and be glad about." (Philippians 4:8 - Phillips)

My daughter's respect for me gave her the confidence that I would lead with the Holy Spirit and not emotions. She trusted that I would be there with the proper guidance in the perfect timing.

We have always had a bond filled with trust and respect. Trust means trusting yourself, your own judgments and trusting others. Trust is the foundation for any relationship. Without it, the relationship will be shaky and will eventually fail. The commencement of my quest with trust with my daughter began with the love, trust, and respect that I had for my grandmother and mother.

When I ponder on respect, what comes to mind is treating people in a positive manner that acknowledges them for who they are and/or what they are doing. Being treated or treating an individual in a dignified manner. Respect is earned and is never just given. You must give respect to receive respect. Meaning when you interact with an individual you treat them with dignity and in a respectful manner as this shows your character as a person. And the respect will be reciprocated. You must always behave in a respectful manner as this reflects on you, your character, integrity, and values of who you are as a person.

No one owes you respect until you have earned it, so there is no such thing as I will give it after they give it to me. That attitude is disrespectful to anyone you interact with as it insinuates that you do not trust them to act accordingly and implies that they "owe" you respect before you will give it. That will cause people to LOSE respect for you or never gain it in the first place. When you meet someone, you give them the benefit of the doubt that they are a respectable individual. Questioning their integrity (respect) before you have even met them and expecting respect to be given without giving it yourself is insulting and condescending to that person and is judging them in a negative light when you know absolutely nothing about them. Thus, to get respect, you must give it. So respectful behavior should just be part of how you function as a person 100% of the time. Everyone deserves a basic amount of respect as an individual until proven otherwise.

It means valuing others points of views. It means being open to being wrong. It means accepting people as they are. It means not dumping on someone because you are having a difficult day. It means being polite and kind - always, because being kind to people is not negotiable. It means not dismissing people because they're different.

Respect is a word describing the mutual relationship between two people. This is something that needs to be cultivated on a person-to-person basis. A mutual relationship cultivated through continuous fair and equitable exchanges of kind and polite interactions, as well as having an understanding and consideration for each other; basic human dignity. This cannot be obtained simply through age, status, experience, knowledge; it must be mutually crafted. Respect is not earned nor given through one man's acts, but through mutual interactions of good will exchanges.

The first people I truly respected were my mother and grandmother. Now, my grandmother brought an entirely unique perspective to the word RESPECT!! I respected my grandmother for the values that she introduced to the family. She brought a deep-rooted concept of trust and respect. I often reflect on my grandmother when it comes to my understanding of biblical teachings and wisdom. Church attendance was a mandatory standard set by my grandmother in the household. Therefore, I learned at an early age the significance of a relationship with God. I grew up learning the Baptist/Christian faith which included a long stretch of praise and worship coupled with a stern message or lesson from the minister.

Weekends also included family time. Family time incorporated a host of fun times and a variety of food selections. I have memories of kickball, football, track, volleyball etc. coupled with barbeques and fish fries. We learned the importance of family, spending time with one another and valuing each other. My grandmother affectionately known as "Mama" earned the respect of the entire family. We were taught to always look out for one another and to always make time for family. I will always respect "Mama" for the lessons that stay with us as we become mothers, fathers, grandmothers, or grandfathers.

I respect "Mama" for her exemplification of hard work. My grandmother was a domestic worker. Quality time with her meant accompanying her to work during the summers. Each of her grandchildren had the opportunity to share in a workday with Mama. My grandmother would pack our lunch, and off we went to catch the bus. Those were precious moments that will never be forgotten. I have a whole different respect for my grandmother, as I witnessed her scrub her customers' floors on her hands and knees. She did it with dignity and grace. She taught me humility. I respect her for the grace that she left with the family. Memories that will never be forgotten.

I had the misfortune of laying my grandmother to rest in 2014. I yearn for her guidance many days and ache with pain because I so deeply miss her presence. I hold on to the talks, the guidance and mentorship. Her home going was an exemplification of her life. Full of energy, virtue, and poise. My mother is much like her in that regard.

When I ponder my respect for my mother, I hope that it measures up to the biblical text, Exodus 20:12. That text says we should, "Honor thy father and thy mother: that thy days may be long upon the land which the LORD thy God giveth thee."

My mother taught me perseverance, resiliency, tenacity, and the importance of setting a strong foundation. I learned the importance of accountability and structure from my mom, and to respect my elders and those around me. I was taught to not listen or indulge in grown folks' conversations. When mom and dad had company, we knew to report to our bedrooms. We were taught to speak to everyone in a room when entering that room. And that the teacher better not have any reason to call her job! We were taught discipline. My mom was my parent and not my friend. You were expected to learn how to cook, clean house, and wash clothes. The respect for who she was and what she poured into my life molded me to be the success story I am today.

I appreciate my mother's toughness, it assisted with my growth. Her big heart taught me to value others. I learned that treating people in a positive manner and acknowledging them for who they are and/or what they are doing shows respect. I learned the importance of treating others in a dignified manner. I learned the importance of earning respect and not assuming it would just be given. You must give respect to receive respect! I represent the very soul of my mother and I respect that as well.

Many may think they understand respect; however, far too many are at a loss. Misunderstandings between diverse cultures, particularly highlighting high-context cultures with low-context cultures. We are now seeing how there can be cultural misunderstandings between groups that are quite similar. Certainly, some of this difference is the result of media manipulation, which spawns not only misunderstanding, but distrust and even hatred because of propaganda. Extreme stereotyping of "the other," also prevents effective cross-group communication, so when communication between groups occurs the messages are highly likely to be misinterpreted.

Much needs to be done to get the right and the left talking without agendas, arrogance and with humility. But once they start, mediators or facilitators are going to be needed to try to reduce misunderstandings and build a groundwork for coexistence and tolerance. This is one area where every individual can make a difference. When we talk to our family members who have different belief systems, for example, take care to use good conflict communication skills among others, instead of escalatory communication.

When I ponder the fruit of respect and disrespect, the following biblical terminology depicts the difference. Scriptures teach us to treat others with respect. Mankind has always failed at this to one degree or another. There are certain kinds of respect that are not appropriate examples of treating others with kindness and dignity. While everybody should be treated with respect or kindness, there are some who do not deserve honor or admiration based on their actions, behaviors, and interactions. Though we should treat such a person with respect, we should not exalt them or their foolish ways. Respect that is mere shallow lip service is also wrong. It is good to say positive, flattering things to others, but never as insincere lip service. Forced respect is also an errant form of respect. One should not use a title, position, or false sense of superiority to manipulate or force someone to respect them. This type of behavior could be considered abusive and narcissistic.

So, what kind of respect is good? First and foremost, we must have respect for God. This is of primary importance because our respect for him leads us to respect others. Honoring Him with substance is due to Him. We should respect fellow Christians. First Timothy 5:1-2 speaks of how we should treat fellow Christians with dignity and respect. The bible in various passages addresses specific relationships and how we should behave in them. We should treat those older than us, especially elders with respect. We should treat mothers and fathers with respect so that we can be blessed with long life. We should treat our neighbors with the respect God gives to us. Husbands should treat their wives with the respect that God gives to the church. The scriptures teach wives to revere their husbands.

Moses' law reflected the timeless principle commanding Israel to respect the aged whether they are related or not. We are to respect them for the life they have lived. Respect for the aged is expressed in such simple courtesies: as waiting for them to speak before speaking. Wisdom demands we especially honor our aged parents. Our children may be watching to see how they should treat us when we are old.

I believe respect is where leadership begins. Supervisors may wear bars on their collar, staff may respect the bars, but that does not mean they respect the person. What is going to make them respect you as a person is whether they trust you. Do they trust you to lead them the right way, to lead them in the right direction? Do you really care? Is it about ego?

Vulnerability is an important trait for a leader to display. I will use the COVID-19 pandemic as an example; although, even before then I would often refer to staff as foot soldiers. I utilize this analogy with line staff because they are the ones that are out on the frontline ensuring tasks are accomplished. Staff facilitate frontline duties; however, they expect leaders to produce solutions. During the pandemic, I had a meeting with my team and shared with them that this level of a pandemic had not been seen before in our lifetime. Further, the pandemic was not local or city situation, but a global situation. So, my vulnerability was that we are shifting through it together. I was humble enough to share that I did not know all the answers, but together we knew the answers we needed. I admitted I had as many questions and uncertainties as they did, but as a team we would shift through those tough times. My sentiments were, although I am your leader, we are going through this together as a team, and yes, I am going to give you direction and yes, I am going to take the lead, but this team has a host of talent sitting at the table and we are all leaders. Sharing an innovative idea with a workable solution sets the tone for a win and that is how we walked through the toughest moments with trust, vulnerability, and - respect.

So, I think the respect also comes with sharing our weaknesses, because we do not know it all. There are things that I am stronger in than the average bear, but there are some things that I still need to work on too. Be vulnerable, lead with respect, trust your team and when you do not know, put it out there to the team.

Admitting to not knowing the solution to a problem as a leader and letting your team know that working the issue through will be a group effort gains respect. A lot of leaders will not necessarily say they know it all, but neither will they share their weaknesses and vulnerabilities with their team. I think it is important in leadership to share your weaknesses. Sometimes a weakness to one is not a weakness to another person. I would say instead of running away from our problems, we must embrace them and as a team, we must learn and share how we are going to get through a trial.

Let's stay with the pandemic scenario. So how do we get through this? That was one of the questions on the table when I met with my team. That was my question to them, how do we get through this? Because we must transition through this. I compared exposure to pepper foam which is a task we must defeat during the academy. In the pepper foam exercise, you are sprayed with the foam. Rather than scatter, you are instructed to latch arms with other cadets and walk through the pepper foam mist together. I wanted the team to digest that concept, because that is exactly what was happening with COVID-19. Because of what we do, the likelihood that we are going to be exposed is extremely high. So, we cannot run away from it, we needed to trust each other enough to lock arms and move through the foam and mist.

When you reap your harvest in your field and forget a sheaf in the field, you shall not go back to get it. It shall be for the sojourner, the fatherless, and the widow, that the Lord your God may bless you in all the work of your hands.

—Deuteronomy 24:19

"It is my wish to fill every moment of my time with some action of the mind which may contribute to the pleasure or the improvement of my fellow creatures."

—*John Quincy Adams*

CHAPTER 5

Giving and Investing of Self

Knowing your staff is paramount to being a great leader. A good leader listens, learns, and then leads (John Maxwell). I had hundreds of staff members reporting to me; so, I could not know all their individual stories. However, it was (and is) imperative that I learn the stories of the teammates closest to me. What impacts them? What makes them lead (or not lead) the way they do? Learning these stories, you have read about several times now means you have to give something. You must give or invest your time for serious conversations. You must invest in being concerned about becoming involved if needed or as invited. You must give an increased level of compassion and empathy to more effectively lead the individual that shows up because of their story.

You may have multiple kids and realize that one of them has extraordinary leadership skills. But that is also the child that is a bit awkward and may be experiencing bullying in school and a lot of teasing from his siblings. So, while he works hard, he often needs a pat on the back. He needs to hear, "Good job!" and when he does not hear, "Good job!" or if you critique something, he does not do well with it. You have realized patience and affirmation are great tools to employ with him. BUT...the other kids think he gets a bit too much of that. Your patience with him frustrates them to no end! They think you spoil him and voice that regularly.

They do not understand that the reason you do those things is because his story does include some ill feelings from them, the kids calling him skinny, or acne-man or whatever. You realize he feels peer pressure a little differently and you want to assure that he knows you believe in him and you want him to believe in himself. In the workplace you will experience grown people who still wear scars from impoverishment, abuse or being bullied. They may excel and lead out project after project, but you still must give that extra dose of affirmation, assurance, and congratulations. And you absolutely should do it. I must understand how to lead and affirm team members from their stories and what their story triggers are. Before you dismiss someone as too needy, try leading from a place of empathy and see how you can allow their strengths to help you sharpen your team. When you know somebody's story, it helps you to lead them. Sit with your team, the ones that work closest to you and in integral positions, find out who they are, what is impacting their thoughts, attitudes, behaviors, and ideals? What are their triggers? What are the things that stimulate them? Learning who is in the room with you not only helps when it comes to giving of yourself to those around you, but it also helps you shape how those you serve can more effectively serve the organization.

The strategies that I use to connect and understand my team are not ones that I practice independently. I sow the skill of investing in the abilities, vision, goals, and stories of others into those around me, so that they can then sow those skills into others. The giving of yourself to others creates a synergetic and productive return on investment. If a leader does nothing else, they should give. I cannot just tell them to give themselves to a cause, their position, their desires and even their challenges, I must share the results. As a leader I want to see them have a steady stream of outcomes. There is enough in all of us to leave something in the people we encounter and do life with. Certainly, if you are a leader but have nobody following you then you are just a person by yourself.

Just because a person reports to you, does not mean they're following you. If you want a team to follow you, they must trust you, they must know you believe in them, and they must respect your criticism. They must know that you will give of your time and experience towards their success.

Investing time and resources into building and supporting team, can be time-consuming. This is especially true if you oversee a medium to large organization Do not let that stop you! You might read that and think, "Oh that is good in theory, but you know what, my inner circle is 10 people and if I am trying to be compassionate in listening to the stories of those 10 people, I am not going to have time to do anything else. I hear what you are saying, but I do not think that is an important leadership skill. Because now you are talking about giving up my time, to be some kind of coach, counselor, or buddy." I feel you. I do. But I say, again, do not let that stop you. In fact, change your mind set. Your 10 minutes with each of the 10 in your circle, may give you insight that can revolutionize something you have oversight over. Investing in others is leadership too. Investing in goals and expectations is paramount to how you all will thrive. There is a reciprocal effect to this giving component of leadership. Your team will become vulnerable and transparent enough to tell you what their expectations of you are. They answer the questions, what are they seeking from me as a leader? I have gained critical thoughts on my success or struggles as the one leading the way.

It is my belief that at the onset of supervising someone, even on a more personal level if you merge a blended family or take over the helm of a ministry you must set the tone in this area. People want to know your expectations and your vision. They want to know that you intend to devise a team vision. They want to know that you are going to give their ideas, thoughts, opinions, and critique careful and sincere consideration, and respect them in the process. You have to share, "Okay, this is what I am looking to do. These are my expectations, and this is what I want from you. This is what I am looking for this team to do."

To create and maintain a trustworthy connection with your team, listening to them is exactly what you do. When you ask what you want from me, most of the time, what you get is, "You know I just want you to be here to support me."

I like to bring everybody's decisions or their thought processes into a final product. If I want to implement something new, the first thing I am going to do is pull the team together, I then propose what I would like to do. If I want to do it but they all are not in total agreement - then I do not do it. I table it for later. I must give

credence to the opinions of stakeholders. It has made leadership
- for me - so much easier and it has given teams the push and
confidence to make quality decisions and suggestions.

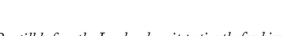

*Be still before the Lord and wait patiently for him;
do not fret when people succeed in their ways, when
they carry out their wicked schemes.*

—Psalm 37:7

"If you can't fly then run, if you can't run then walk, if you can't walk then crawl, but whatever you do you have to keep moving forward."

—Martin Luther King Jr.

CHAPTER 6

Determination and its Friends

When I was a young mother on welfare, not only did I know that there was more than that label. I also knew there was more in me. I knew that I had already developed some characteristics and traits that I could powerfully use somewhere. I also knew that I would not rest until I figured out what that something was – not just for my daughter and I, but for my extended family. I was determined and I remained determined to excel in my current moment and in what will manifest in my next steps, whatever they may be.

Building one's determination, starts with confidence. Knowing you could do anything that you put your mind to, should be the prompt to go for whatever your mind challenges you to achieve. Setting goals for yourself that seem bigger than everything around you. Holding yourself accountable even when everything is falling apart, or tragedy or crisis hits builds your determination. In the most challenging times is when you assess the measure of your leadership. In an interview, Bishop Jakes said, "We're going to see who the true leaders are. Problems are basically opportunities for you to show who you really are as a leader."

I hold myself accountable to those things God assigns to me and those things I have assigned and assumed for myself. If I cannot be honest and diligent in what I have given my word to; then why would I expect anyone else to bring those things in the door with them when they must work with me. Determination is that muscle that you use to push up against distractions, disappointments, and unbelievable tasks. It is a muscle that you use to pull you up from those relationships, obligations, partnerships, positions, and similar things that seemed to be more disparaging than anything else. Determination tests your mettle when it comes to how much of self you are willing to pour into what is out there for you to obtain. Determination builds resilience.

Oxford Dictionaries defines resilience as: the capacity to recover quickly from difficulties; toughness: The ability of a substance or object to spring back into shape; elasticity." Psychology

Today reports that "Resilience is the psychological quality that allows some people to be knocked down by the adversities of life and come back at least as strong as before. Rather than letting difficulties, traumatic events, or failure overcome them and drain their resolve, highly resilient people find a way to change course, emotionally heal, and continue moving toward their goals."

Resilience partnered with determination activates that I see it and I will obtain it spark within. I knew to get to certain places in my life, at work, at home, in relationships, and everything I do, I had to not be thwarted by those things that could stop me. Resilience and determination start with a mindset. From the beginning of this body of work, I declared that everything you are holistically, and for purposes of this book, begins with where and who you are spiritually and mentally. Your mind must be wired to re-ignite after every infraction because you have a purpose to walk out. Everything rises and falls on your mindset. You must persevere, and you must have the tenacity to do.

You must also know your why. Why are you here? Why are you in that family? Why are you in that marriage, church, job? Why are you seeking that position, that promotion, that level of elevation? When the societal definitions and expectations are stripped away – what is your why? And your why – in case no one ever told you - must be more valuable than the money. Even though I know money plays a role, THE WHY must be so much bigger than the financial gain. Money is temporal and its value can be fickle. You must have passion to make the difference. You must want to leave a legacy; you must want to share your talents. You must value others. You must persevere. You must push even when you do not want to push, even when you are scared. And it must all come from your WHY.

When I look at leadership, when people hear leadership, they think about rank or position. I do not look at leadership that way. I look at leadership as what that person brings to the table, whatever we are dealing with at that time when we are having that seat at the table, that is who the leader is, and the leader can be the janitor at that moment. If that is not my forte, then I need to yield the floor to the janitor. That is the leader at that moment, and I need to know my place and be confident within my own skin to know that just because the janitor is leading, they are taking nothing away from me. I can be that way and a true leader should be that way because it is not about the position, it is about the why.

Looking at leadership, there are identifiable leadership flaws and positive skills that will show openly. During various crises I have seen some people step up and be there. We did not have to tell them what to do. They came to the table with suggestions and resolutions not just to make their jobs easier but to help the agency and the staff. They did not think about themselves. We had foot soldiers that were not leaders by rank but were leaders by actions. The largest crisis we faced (COVID-19) exemplified how determination to not allow one of the largest law enforcement agencies in South Florida to be knocked down, highlighted the resilience of a force. Those are leaders to me. They did not allow fear to encourage them to not show up or retreat.

As a leader, I had to remind myself to be determined to be accountable to my duty. I did not have a choice to retreat even though I had fears, even though I had uncertainty. I had a duty to step up and have a seat at the table and to build tables with other leaders and ensure staff and leadership could perform their job duties effectively and safely. It was a challenge. But I was determined to do it. And my determination fed off the determination of others and vice versa. We had to get up and be on the battlefield with the rest of the troops. That is leadership!!! "The human capacity for burden is like bamboo – far more flexible than you'd ever believe at first glance." Author Jodi Picoult, My Sister's Keeper.

During my journey in law enforcement, I had to learn how to lead difficult people, scared people, and weak people. You do not have the right to choose who you lead. You must lead those you like, but more importantly you must lead those who oppose you. That does not stop you. It increases your determination. I had to lead people that I knew were not necessarily on my team though they were on the team. I had to lead people who I knew did not like me. I did not and I do not have a choice to say, "Okay, well I could lead A because A likes me and they have the same vision that I have but I'm not going to lead B because B doesn't like me;" or, "B is talking about me" or, "B is giving me a hard time." I must lead A and B just the same. And I must do it to be resilient in my why.

Leadership is not easy, and you must master leading difficult people. This will help you become a better leader. You must understand the difference between constituents, confidants, and comrades. All have a special role in your leadership journey. You do not want everybody to be a confidant. You need your constituents. Some people are to be with you at a certain place or at a certain time. So, there is some people who I know probably did not care for me, but because we have the same common goal, we tackled situations together. I do not take it personal because everybody is not meant to be your confidant. Each of these three types of people will increase your resilience, fine tune your termination, and enhance your vulnerability as a leader.

I have a duty. God has allowed me to wear leadership bars and I was fortunate to have them, so it was imperative that I lead and guide the troops. While leading them, there was a responsibility to ultimately guide with discipline and a solid work ethic. These were instilled in me during my youth and so being disciplined comes naturally for me. In leadership, I am glad it does. It is something that I can model in personal and professional relationships consistently and comfortably.

I always was the child that if my parents said do something, I did it. I did not really resist too much. My family said they always knew I was going to be a police officer even as a little girl. They said they knew I was going to be in some type of law enforcement or military. That is something that came natural for me. It was not something I had to really work at. Of course, I have had to work on discipline and self-accountability as I have progressed through life, but it was not a big struggle. Because of my discipline, I have also always held myself accountable, always had goals - even when I did not really know the meaning of goals. I would write little affirmations and be determined that what I wrote was what was going to happen. That practice continues, of course, with my journaling. When I write it down, I am reminded of my why, I am focused on believing in what I wrote, I am determined to work towards it and even though I am wise enough to know that distractions, deflections, and all things contrary might come my way, I am always determined that I will overcome.

For no good tree bears bad fruit, nor again does a bad tree bear good fruit, for each tree is known by its own fruit. For figs are not gathered from thorn bushes, nor are grapes picked from a bramble bush. The good person out of the good treasure of his heart produces good, and the evil person out of his evil treasure produces evil, for out of the abundance of the heart his mouth speaks.

—Luke 6:43–45

"Average leaders raise the bar on themselves; good leaders raise the bar for others; great leaders inspire others to raise their own bar."

—*Orrin Woodward*

CHAPTER 7

Mentorship

Mentorship is a collaboration that few secure these days. However, I believe that a mentor is one of life's necessities to lessen those bumps in the road of growth and success. In his book "Leadership Gold" John Maxwell offers, "A mentor is someone who teaches, guides and lifts you up by virtue of his or her experience and insight. They are usually someone a little farther ahead of you on the path—though that does not always mean they are older! A mentor is someone with a head full of experience and heart full of generosity that brings those things together in your life."

When I look for a mentor, there are some must haves: courage, humility, strength, trust, character, transparency, and accountability. Why is courage my first choice? I think being courageous is a big part of being a leader. You cannot be a leader that is easily shifted, or that is easily broken. Powerhouse motivator and author Les Brown says, "Go where there is no path and leave a trail. The higher you soar; the more obstacles will come your way." THAT IS LEADERSHIP and the kind of magic I want to glean from! You must also be a leader that is courageous enough to confront your fears.

Mentoring is one of many opportunities I enjoy. It must be a mutual connection though. When I offer or when I am asked to mentor others, I have a specific type of person in mind. I look for those who are looking to excel, those that are looking to lead. Sometimes they possess qualities that just need to be built upon. When I see that, I like to help them along the way. For instance, I am shy, and I supervised a sergeant who I believed had immense potential, but just like me she was extremely shy. I saw myself in her. Usually that is what we do as leaders. We mentor and coach individuals that exhibit characteristics or struggles that we faced during our leadership journey. I visualized this supervisor as a good leader, therefore I really wanted to coach her, guide her, build her confidence, make her more courageous, and I did. I worked with her to challenge her to want to challenge herself.

I look for those type of individuals, people that I feel have great leadership potential. I know they can do better but sometimes they do not see their potential. They need someone to push them along the way and that is what leadership is all about. The best leaders had great mentors. They are the great foot soldiers, but they do not think that they will be good leaders. Sometimes in life we need someone to see our potential. To believe in us. To see beyond our flaws. To see beyond our fears. To trust us. Sometimes in life, we just need someone to help push us to become better. I relate this to expanding our values. And for these reasons, I believe that mentorship is imperative.

Although I am a mentor, I also have a mentor. I constantly want to extent value to others through mentorship. I look at this process as an oil change. I constantly give my oil to others, but I also require a refuel so that I can effectively encourage others. I call this two-way mentorship. I also look for mentees to seek me and ask me to be their mentor because if they are looking for a mentor, they know that they do have qualifications or qualities that can get them where they want to be. Plus, they are looking for leaders that are strong in areas where they know they need improvement. As I continue to mentor, I am dedicated to the mentorship I receive. It makes me a better person overall. I mentioned that I have hands-on mentors and mentors that I study. My hands-on mentors include Chief Constance Stanley of the Lauderhill Police Department (a city in Broward County, Florida), and Real Estate and Contracting Entrepreneur Brenda Riggins. It is easy to become stagnant during your leadership journey; therefore, you require others that will push you, believe in you, and add value to you. You need those to share their respective trials, tribulations, and the hurdles they have crossed over or endured. You need that enrichment. My study mentors include: John Maxwell, Grant Cardone, Les Brown, Bishop T.D. Jakes, Warren Buffett, Jim Collins, Stephen Covey, and Zig Ziglar. These are people that I have never met, yet they have profound influence on my life.

Because mentorship is vital to refining one's professional and even personal definitions; I encourage both mentor and mentee to prepare for their quality time together. Prior to meeting with my mentors, I prepare questions. I value and appreciate their time and want to ensure that I take advantage of every second of the experience. Every month, I try to take someone of influence out. I strive to have a lunch, brunch, or dinner with somebody who can mentor me. I have questions setup for them and then send them a nice little thank you letter. Now, although we enjoy the meals, we are deep in conversations that can at times, be life changing. An example of questions I may ask are, "What are some of your struggles?" or "What are some of your fears?" One question that I try to ask all of them is, "Tell me about a situation or something you had to deal with that could have changed your entire career, how did you manage the situation and what was the outcome?"

I expect everybody on my team to be mentoring someone. I do not want us to ever get too busy that we cannot help someone build themselves up. Whether they are mentoring youth, battered women, ex-offenders, those struggling with chronic illnesses – does not matter. What matters is that they are holding a hand and pulling someone up. Everybody should have somebody that they are helping to be a better version of themself.

I think far too many folks do not have a mindset to help. And that is what you are doing. You are helping, and you are not getting an extra paycheck for doing it, and often there is no special recognition. We must move away from the "If it ain't about me or if I can't shine, I'm not doing that" way of thinking.

Unfortunately, a growing number of leaders have that mindset. I have had some people tell me they will not seek out mentees, they will mentor someone only if they ask them. And the potential mentee must have certain qualifications to be mentored. See I will not do that. If a person comes to me, I will not tell someone that I am not going to mentor them. I am going to mentor anybody who wants to be better. I am going to help them to do better until they show me that they do not want better. Or until they show me that they lack initiative to do better or have some other ulterior motive.

As a leader who mentors, you should be challenged and invigorated by the possibility of creating someone who might end up leading you. That says something awesome about you as a leader. I tell my team all the time, "I expect you to be my boss one day." Then I know I have done my job. "No one gets to the top alone. We all have help. It is why I have made mentoring such a crucial part of my growth—and it is why I mentor people along the way. It is the inspiration for my Maximum Impact Mentoring call each month, and the reason I continue to write and speak to audiences each year. I want to help as many people as possible become all they can be," wrote John Maxwell.

Now it happened in the process of time that the king of Egypt died. Then the children of Israel groaned because of the bondage, and they cried out; and their cry came up to God because of the bondage. So, God heard their groaning, and God remembered His covenant with Abraham, with Isaac, and with Jacob. And God looked upon the children of Israel, and God acknowledged them.

—Exodus 2:23–25

"*Growth demands a temporary surrender of security. It may mean giving up familiar but limiting patterns, safe but unrewarding work, values no longer believed in, and relationships that have lost their meaning.*"

—*John Maxwell*

CHAPTER 8

Can your Birdies Fly?

There is a biblical passage that is often taught regarding raising children. I am opening with that passage to shake up the way you might be thinking about encouraging your birdies to leave the nest and fly away. Psalm 127:3-5 (ESV) reads: "Behold, children are a heritage from the Lord, the fruit of the womb a reward. Like arrows in the hand of a warrior are the children of one's youth. Blessed is the man who fills his quiver with them! He shall not be put to shame when he speaks with his enemies in the gate." This scripture teaches us that those in our care are to be trained and conditioned so that we are aimed towards destiny and released, they will land where they are supposed to. But the arrow must come out of the quiver.

When others flourish where you have been helpful in their journey, it says a lot about you as the head. On the opposite side, if you are a leader and nobody around you is moving or advancing, I think it says a lot about your leadership. Now that is just my thing, I think if you are leading people and nobody is being promoted, nobody is going back to school, nobody is accomplishing anything, then what's going on? A great leader pushes those around them and assists them with transitioning into leadership roles. Pushing potential leaders to excel does not lessen your position. "The position," according to John Maxwell, "doesn't make the leader; the leader makes the position."

Although great leadership helps to transform and prepare others for growth, for some leaders, this may be a downfall. Let me explain. Some leaders may see growth in staff as a loss. When one begins to learn, build, and flourish, they may - in some cases – leave to grab better opportunities. However, there are those who relish in the growth of others. Even if it means possibly having to restructure the team or hire a new team member, that is part of the excitement of change.

Some leaders may think they are doing a good thing by building a team of people with no ambition beyond their current position. They are comfortable in a solid and steady position and environment of people who are all waiting to retire. I get it, helping others grow, encouraging them to go after promotions or lateral moves, and not worry about them leaving is disconcerting. And when you are trying to stay caught up on your job duties pushing someone to higher heights could be taxing. But the reward for clapping and cheering your team on is indescribable. When I saw one of my staff walk across the stage and become a sergeant, I cried like I was a proud parent. His success and his elevation - elevated me. Maxwell's teaching was illuminated for me. "Great leaders stand behind the team to push them along the way, alongside them show the way and at times in front of them to pave the way. Most important, is that they are always there guiding!"

When the collective around you progresses, it affirms that what you have instilled in them; mental conditioning, discipline, determination, resilience, character, mentoring, and professional development has responded to your why and lit a fire under theirs.

Very truly I tell you, whoever believes in me will do the works I have been doing, and they will do even greater things than these, because I am going to the Father.

—*John 14:12*

"Everybody can be great... because anybody can serve. You don't have to have a college degree to serve. You don't have to make your subject and verb agree to serve. You only need a heart full of grace. A soul generated by love."

—*Martin Luther King, Jr.*

CHAPTER 9

Succession

"Success comes when they (leaders) lead followers to do great things for them. But a legacy is created only when leaders put their people into a position to do great things without them. The legacy of successful leaders lives on through the people they touch along the way. The only things you can change permanently are the hearts of the people you lead." (John Maxwell, Good Leaders Ask Great Questions)

I keep telling myself, "This is a preparatory stage for something so much bigger." God is preparing us for something so much bigger but if we are going to have bigger then there must be something in place to make sure if where we are is someone else's bigger we have prepared them for it. Preparing the next shift – so to speak - is interesting and only the strong will come out on the other side victoriously, without their ego yelling and with their arrogance intact. Plus, preparing the next shift means you have determined that the good of the whole body is more important than the part you represent. Which is why succession is so vital in our personal and professional lives.

Bridgespan.org summarizes succession in this matter: "Succession planning is the process of identifying and developing new leaders to succeed current leaders. At its best, it is a proactive and systematic investment in building a pipeline of leaders within an organization and identifying strong external candidates, so that when transitions are necessary, leaders at all levels are ready to act."

I am an advocate of a succession plan. Estate planning is a succession plan of sorts. Lawyers and family members use the various components to spell out a person's legacy. A succession plan builds on that in a professional sense. Part of leaving your legacy is leaving your agency or organization in a better position than when you came. True leaders do not want things to change once they retire or move on to something different. You do not want things to be stagnant or fail because you are not present. You want to share your values, global thinking, and strategies that will make the agency better because you want your legacy to continue. Your legacy remains by sharing your values with others that are going to fill your shoes. You do not want them to do it exactly the way you did, but you do want them to have some of your wisdom and tools. Everyone should be preparing someone to walk in their shoes.

People are reluctant to share their talents because they feel like the person is going to take their job. That is why a lot of people do not like succession planning, per se, because they feel intimidated by somebody younger coming in and doing the job better. I just have a different concept as it relates to that. Why wouldn't you want somebody younger to come in and do it better? Why wouldn't you want them to come in and take some of what you have and what they have and make the agency, company, ministry, organization soar? Why wouldn't you want that? You should be preparing the upgraded version of you. I do not care if it is the janitor. I am going to show the janitor what to do, I am going to teach him or her something and I am hoping that he or she can also teach me something. My belief is that there is something to learn from everybody. You must focus on the lesson. You must allow the lessons to steer the next generation of leaders. That janitor you teach today may be the most profound chief executive officer the company has ever been steered by five years from your encounter.

Succession planning is not necessarily the boss teaching the subordinate, it is the boss being confident within self and knowing that they can learn from everybody and everybody on the team brings something to the team. This is a valuable part of succession plan. First, meeting with the specific employee that you have earmarked for promotional greatness because succession planning is also about relationship. You cannot just pick somebody and say, "Oh okay, I'm going to push you to be a leader." The employee may not want to be a leader, but they may want to obtain a college degree, or they may want to transfer to a different department. Succession planning is not only filling your shoes, but also helping someone to live their dream or to excel to what they dream about becoming.

I think you must build a relationship. You must build that trust. You must obtain that person's expectations from you. I would ask them, "How can I help you get to where you want to be? What traits do I have or what do you need from me to help you be a better you, even if that better you is staying where you are? How can I make you the best version of you in your career and personal life?" It is just having the conversation, and once I have the conversation, we would jot down some expectations and feedback. I encourage them to interview me, we would come back to the table and we would do follow up. I provide them with a timeline. For instance, if they want to go back to school, I will provide them with a date for acquiring transcripts. Or perhaps I would have them research why they want to pursue a specific career. I may ask, "Why do you want to get promoted/why do you want to become a leader?"

If I ask why you want to be a sergeant; and they cannot tell me why, I may be left feeling they probably just want to do it for the money and or prestige. There is more to leadership than money. I have had people say, "I want to show my child that I can be a leader, that I can lead, that I can persevere. I want to show them that you could be anything you want to be in life if you put your mind to it." It is imperative that I dive into that person's mindset to see exactly how I can contribute to wherever they want to go. That is the relationship of succession.

Some people that I mentor for succession is not necessarily about them getting promoted. It may be to help them with their finances, it may be to help them become a homeowner. It may be to help them build their credit. When it comes to succession planning, there are so many different variables. Succession planning is about helping people and using your talents to help people become a better version of them and whatever that is, is up to the person to determine.

As a leader in the position to prepare a person for succession, it is critical that your plan is built on the premise of not wanting to leave any position in the hands of someone who is not ready or willing to continue to move the organization, company, or position forward in a positive way. Some people may say, "Well I don't care what happens to the agency when I leave, I do not care about this place falling apart." That is not leadership. That is selfish. A leader organically will want their department, area, or company to continue to soar in their absence. They want people to shine. They want people to move up the leadership ladder and or excel.

Every organization - whether it is spiritual, law enforcement, etc., should have some type of succession plan in place and in fact, managers and supervisors in those organizations should have the same. I do not care what the position is, everyone should be showing somebody how to perform at a higher level. That performance should be geared toward leadership within that position. I asked my accountant as I was getting my taxes completed, "Are you showing your daughter how to do this one day to carry on your legacy?" She smiled and responded, "Absolutely." Some people do not think about it. They do not really think, "I need to be coaching someone to do my job. I need to be training someone in this area. I need to be building someone in this area." I do not believe they think about legacy in that way.

As I think about succession opportunities in the areas I am assigned to, I remind myself that whomever I have earmarked has a say so in the process. It is so easy for me to see a staff member and notice their strengths and weaknesses and make an approximate decision on how they will probably need to move forward professionally. However, that is not my call. I have to be comfortable and intentional and ask a staff member what they foresee as their next step, and honestly, as I look at a succession plan for them, I have to ask, "Okay, Sherea, what's next for you then? Or "Where do you want to go from here?" I cannot get stagnant, and I do not want to get to a place that because of the busyness of my job or the busyness of what I have going on around me that I do not continue to develop as a person. What do I want to do next? Do I want to go to the next level? What is that next level for me? Will I say yes to it? I will ALWAYS say yes; I am going to go wherever God needs me to go. One of my affirmations is that I touch everyone in this universe. And, though it may sound like a supersized quest, I believe that I will. Then my questions become, what do I want to do in the community? What do I want to be involved in outside of law enforcement? Who can I impact through my purpose and my why? Perhaps my succession plan will unfold through my journaling. Now may be the time to incorporate that, what is next for me Lord? Reveal to me what you want me to do next? That could be quite unnerving since what I begin to journal about does not take long to manifest.

This Book of the Law shall not depart from your mouth, but you shall meditate on it day and night, so that you may be careful to do according to all that is written in it. For then you will make your way prosperous, and then you will have good success.

—Joshua 1:8

"*Believe in yourself. You are braver than you think, more talented than you know, and capable of more than you imagine.*"

—*Roy T. Bennett*

CHAPTER 10

Stay Teachable

"Time is precious and irreversible, and we must keep this in mind. We need to continually challenge ourselves to improve in every area of our lives—both personally and professionally."

—Dr. Wayne Dyer

From the beginning of my career one thing was certain, I would remain teachable because I would always strive for more. Even with a steady road of advancements I continued to train. Part of my varied responsibilities have involved monitoring, and coordinating special projects ensuring compliance with the standards and ordinances. I am also often in meetings with higher-ranging officers and community as well as political leaders. Thus, learning new policies, measures, strategies, and efforts to stay ahead of the mark is necessary. It remains imperative that I hone my skills in the areas of compliance, safety, management, multitasking, facilitation, interpersonal/written communication, detail orientation and so much more. If I remain teachable and I continue to study to show myself approval, then I am always ready to serve and walk through doors that are opened for me or someone with my qualifications and skillset. Even after obtaining a Master of Science in Criminal Justice in 2006, I acquired several certifications in Leadership Development to facilitate my effectiveness and productivity.

A good leader should make training, professional and personal development part of their lifestyle and success rituals. There is always more to learn even in your position or in a field that you have worked in for decades. Innovation creates new systems, technology and applications or software.

Beyond the academic and professional charge to remain teachable, is to also do so when it comes to whether you can learn in the workplace, or even in your home from those who may be younger, in a subordinate position, or a beginner. Their position does not dictate that there is nothing they can teach you. The person you refuse to respect or listen to might hold the key to the very things that continues to stomp you. Theologian and author Saint Augustine said: "Do you wish to rise? Begin by descending. Are you planning a tower that will pierce the clouds? Lay first the foundation of humility. So, how teachable are you?

Brian Brown, writing for WorshipLife, identified "5 Signs of an Un-Teachable Spirit". Those signs are:

1. "You get offended when someone tries to teach you something you already know.
2. You pretend you already know what is being taught, even when you do not.
3. You cannot take instruction from those in lower positions.
4. You feel certain tasks are beneath you, so you do not need to learn them.
5. You try to "one-up" the one giving instruction by proving you know more than they do."

Do any of those things step on your toes? If so, you have some work to do. An un-teachable person has closed off a significant part of the world, including the world they function in. "Ego makes a leader unteachable and unapproachable – two leadership killers." – Ty Bennett, Author of Beware of Your Ego

How to Build a table of great leaders:
Transparency
Accountability
Open and Honest Communication
Honesty
Humility
Adding Value to Others

For an overseer, as God's steward, must be above reproach. He must not be arrogant or quick-tempered or a drunkard or violent or greedy for gain, but hospitable, a lover of good, self-controlled, upright, holy, and disciplined. He must hold firm to the trustworthy word as taught, so that he may be able to give instruction in sound doctrine and to rebuke those who contradict it.

—Titus 1:7-9

"Do not go where the path may lead, go instead where there is no path and leave a trail."

—*Ralph Waldo Emerson*

Meet the Author

"I am going to lead until I leave this life!"

—*Sherea Green*

Sherea Green's law enforcement career began in 1993 at South Florida Reception Center, Florida Department of Corrections as a Classification Transfer Clerk. In 1995, she went on to become a Correctional Officer and in 1997 transferred to the Broward Sheriff's Office as a Detention Deputy. As a deputy, she worked at the Main Jail Bureau and North Broward Bureau in the Law Library, disciplinary confinement, the Infirmary, and with mentally challenged inmates. While stationed in the Law Library she had the opportunity to assist with the implementation of the department's On-Line Law Library Services. This is an internet-based legal research web-site accessible by Legal Services Specialists for the retrieval of inmate research requests. In 2005, she was promoted to the rank of Sergeant and was assigned to the Main Jail Bureau. At this facility, she served as a Support Sergeant, supervised maximum custody inmates and juveniles. In 2011, she was promoted to the rank of Lieutenant where she was the Shift Commander at the Joseph V. Conte Detention Facility, North Broward Bureau, and Main Jail Bureau. In October of 2014, she was assigned as the Acting Executive Officer in Central Intake Bureau and supervised pre-magistrate holdings, court activities, confinement status, releasing, hospital details, and transportation of inmates. In January of 2015, she progressed to Executive Officer and worked at the North Broward Bureau and Paul Rein Detention Facility. In

February of 2017, she was promoted to the rank of Captain and was assigned to the Main Jail Bureau. In December 2019, there was another step up the career ladder with a promotion to the rank of Major. She served as Assistant Director of South Operations, inclusive of the Main Jail Bureau, Courts Security, Central Intake Bureau, and the Juvenile Assessment Center. As Sherea served in this executive level position, she supervised a growing number of sworn and civilian staff. Additionally, she had the responsibility of overseeing the fiscal management of the Department of Detention - South Operations.

An overview of her academic achievements encompasses degrees in Criminal Justice, an Associate in Science at Miami Dade College North Campus and Bachelor of Science from Florida International University in 2002 and 2004, respectively. Sherea earned her Master of Science in Criminal Justice from Florida International University in 2006 and was cross certified as a Law Enforcement Officer in that same year. In 2011, she completed the Executive Leadership Program at Nova Southeastern University in Davie, Florida. In 2012, she attended Leadership North Broward sponsored by The Pompano Beach Chamber of Commerce. In 2013, she completed The National Jail Leadership Command Academy in Huntsville, Texas as well as the Florida General Instructor Techniques Course. In 2016, she completed the Southern Police Institute at the University of Louisville, "Command Officers Development Course". Sherea is a Certified Jail Services Inspector with The Florida Model Jail Standards Committee and a Certified Jail Manager, which is recognized by The Jail Manager Certification Commission (JMCC) and the American Jail Association (AJA).

Sherea is an Adjunct Instructor for Broward College Institute of Criminal Justice Studies. Setting ambitious standards for herself, she maintains active and supportive membership with The Florida Sheriff's Association, National Sheriff's Association, The American Correctional Association, The National Organization of Black Law Enforcement (NOBLE), American Jail Association (AJA), International Association of Women, National Association of Professional Women and serves as First Vice President for The Broward County Business and Professional Women's Network. Sherea also serves as Vice President for Healthy Hire Healthy Retire, a 501C3 nonprofit assisting first responders, veterans, and family members in need. With the mental health crisis affecting so many first responders and their families her hope is to make a substantial impact within her local community.

Not only has Sherea been a leader in her career, but she also extends an olive branch to her community by serving as a Mentor for the 93rd Street Community Baptist Church Mentoring Princess Ministry. She is trusted in her stewardship and serves as Treasurer for Moms2Moms/58 Foundation Inc.

Her belief is that "A true leader should showcase the team's efforts but stand in the shadows during the victory!" Therefore, in March 2015, the basis of her philosophical stance was recognized by Barry University during Women in Leadership Week – "Honoring Women that Serve in the Community". She was also acknowledged by State Representative Gwyndolen Clarke-Reed District 92 on August 30, 2015 as a Pacesetter for Women in Law Enforcement. The Broward County Business and Professional Women's Network presented Sherea with the High Achievers Award on May 22, 2016 during their 12th Annual Founder's Day Scholarship Luncheon.

Sherea is also a licensed Real Estate Agent and Investor. Her goal is to leave a legacy by touching everyone in this universe by utilizing a combination of her skills, talents, and purpose. Her mantras are, "It's better to give than to receive. Giving begins the receiving process," and "Average leaders raise the bar on themselves; good leaders raise the bar for others; great leaders inspire others to raise their own bar." – Orrin Woodard.

"The best leadership starts
with self-leadership."

Lightning Source UK Ltd.
Milton Keynes UK
UKHW020636100621
385271UK00011B/741